# THE ART OF BEING HALF ASLEEP IN AN OVERSATURATED ROOM

Julia—

I hope you enjoy the poems! Thank you so much for your support!

P.S: you're a great sister to Kiersten ☺

♡ Malia

# The Art of Being Half Asleep in an Oversaturated Room

Malia Robinson

MMR

*dedications*

for the people who love rainstorms,
open-ended questions, and meeting strangers

for Mr. Morris,
thank you for teaching me so much about writing
and even more about life

for Ms. Deorocki,
thank you for showing me the connection that can
be brought about by literature in times of isolation

for Ms. Murphy,
thank you for teaching me the importance of reflection
and of course, how to win an argument

for my mother, father, family & friends
thank you for your never-ending love and support

# Contents

# the city (i.)

# the window

The fractured lights of the city
burn through darkness
and reflect across window glass
as you with your wide eyes
watch the wandering people
and wonder.
Night has fallen
and spread indigo from her hands
across the sky like water.
And still you sit on your knees
in front of the window,
fogging it with your breath.
Come, little one, rest your head
and be warm
away from the window.
No, you reply.
You would rather watch the people.
Because the woman passing the window now,
with her tangled, graying hair and the

torn and yellowed parchment skin
is begging you to listen to her story.


I sit down next to you,
and see her walking through the dark
with unsure footsteps
and broken eyes.
You say that the woman is on her way to save a life
and the life she is saving
is her own.
I say she is buying tea from the market
to bring home to her six children,
or to warm her skin and block out the noise of New York.
And you,
you say she never had children,
you say she lives alone.
Her whole life she remained
lost.
But you tell me that maybe tonight
she will cover her scars with a blanket of hope.
Maybe tonight
she will trade
cigarettes for a pen
and write her story down on paper
so we can read it.
The woman's unsteady feet
have carried her around a corner
and out of sight.

You, with your round blush cheeks
and flaxen hair,
continue to watch for more
souls to pass by.
Your eyes are glued to the glass.
Come, my dear, and go to sleep,
I say.
And you do,
on my shoulder
in front of the window.
I still practice
the lessons you have taught me.
A young girl like you
of only twelve
told me to watch the people.
Told me to listen.
Watch the people,
and you will learn about them
and you will learn
about yourself.
I hear the city shift
in its grand velvet armchair
as it waits to hear the story
of the woman we saw that night.
As it waits to hear the story
of the woman who saved herself.

# nightfall

There's a moment
when the sun shakes and hesitates,
and the light is pulled from the sky,
color stripped from a canvas.
There's a moment
when the shadows have dimensions
and move the streets like liquid darkness.
There's a moment
after the clouds blush
and the birds fall
and wind takes their place,
creeping through the town
like a question,
and the air tastes like memories
that cannot be remembered,
so everyone stays
inside.
There's a moment
when the pavement turns into stars,

and the streetlights are fireflies,
and the people are ghosts.
When you can feel lost words
hanging on the breeze
in every shaft of moonlight,
and every animal stops
to listen.
I wonder if you
would stop to listen
too.

# teddy bear

It was the type of gray afternoon
where the fog clings to everything,
like a cold promise that cannot be kept
but still hides in every corner
and hovers overhead.
It was the type of afternoon
that doesn't have room for hope,
only for the bland bustle of business
and the discomfort of quiet arguments.
As I stood on the platform
waiting for the train,
I could feel the fog searching through my jacket
and surrounding my head
like a ghostly halo.
My eyes wandered
to a lonely wooden bench
at the far end of the platform,
where a young girl sat
clutching a brown stuffed bear.

She was alone
and watched me from behind the bear's fur.
That's when she tilted her head,
flaxen braids swinging,
and lifted a small hand
to wave.
Young girls
shouldn't be alone on train platforms
so I walked through the fog to sit beside her.
I asked her where her parents were.
She smiled, and her wide emerald eyes
full of youth and light and promise
met mine,
as gray as the fog
and many years older.
She didn't respond,
but asked where the train would take me.
Her voice was too delicate and too sweet
to be talking to a phantom like me.
I told her the train would take me to an office
where I would address envelopes
and manage money,
the center of our world.
She frowned
and squeezed her teddy bear,
and told me that didn't sound like
life.
The fog shimmered with her innocence

and she leaned in to regard me
with her questioning eyes.
She asked me
where I wanted the train to take me,
and I couldn't
find
the answer.
I asked her where the train was taking her,
and she stared at me through the haze of mist.
She told me that the train would bring her
to see the world.
She told me I should try it too,
and placed the stuffed bear
with mismatched button eyes
and worn, ragged fur
into my lap.
I told her that she should take her bear back,
they were for young girls like her
and not old men like me.
She told me that teddy bears
were made for everyone,
that maybe the bear could use a new friend
and maybe I could too.
I stared across the platform,
at the people rushing
breathing
typing
and existing

but not living.
I looked down at the hope
in my hands,
the life of a young girl
in one small, furry toy
and smiled.
I turned, to give the bear back
to the little girl,
but she was gone,
had disappeared
into the fog,
and the wooden bench was cold
as if the child
with a wish to see the world
and words so full of life
had never sat beside me.

# the café

The sharp wind has pushed all of us in through the door
and out of the bitter night.
I watch the rain paint the darkened windows in fluid
patterns, and listen to the river of voices around me.
Some laugh, some whisper, and some stay silent.
The room is bathed in soft yellow light,
casting away the wind and shielding us from the darkness.
My fingers are wrapped around a pen
and hover over a blank page,
but I never touch the paper with ink.
Instead I notice the girl walking in,
shaking raindrops from her coat.
She walks to a table in the corner,
as if to hide from the rest of us.
Her hair is curled into perfect waves
that wilt under the weight of the rain.
Her nails are painted a deep red,
but they chip when she bites them.
A single tear falls from her lashes

and glides slowly down her cheek,
shimmering in the lamplight.
She doesn't wipe it away,
she lets it drift until it slips from her skin
and disappears.
She is a glass doll with an invisible crack,
the smooth porcelain of her face
has a spider web of broken lines.
I bring my pen to the paper and draw a line,
watching it curve and twist across the page.
The pen is dark and bland, for I have no need for color
when I could watch the world
paint a canvas full of colors before me.
My paper is liquid and flows as my hand sweeps across it,
brushing a stroke of darkness through the white.
The blankness of my mind has been replaced by questions
as I wonder about the girl in the corner.
Why is she hiding,
and why is she crying,
and why is she broken?
I pull my hand from the paper,
watching my drawings move across the page.
My coffee is cold as the night beside me.
On the other side of the cafe,
a boy is sitting alone
with a jacket draped around his shoulders
and his legs folded beneath him.
His face is downcast,

and he is writing in a worn journal.
He doesn't notice the girl in the corner,
nobody does.
A warm shadow of peace is cast across his face,
and the lamplight frames his skin in gold
as he whispers the words he writes.
He is wrapped in his thoughts,
and doesn't look up
when a cup of warm tea is delivered to his side.
I wonder what he is writing.
Is it a letter,
or a poem,
or a memory?
Ink flows across my paper,
creating a story without words
as my wrist caves and wanders along the page
creating thoughtless lines and shapes.
The storm knocks on the window,
asking to be let in,
but the room is warm with the
silent thoughts of strangers.
I have saved their stories on the paper,
and my hand drops the pen.
The cafe is full of unspoken words
and I want to remember them all.

# the taxi

He knows
that the streets are alive at night
and that too many left turns
could lead into the dark mouth
of reality,
and that too many right turns
lead into the depths of all that is unreal.
But he loves the world at night,
and he loves how the streets stay awake
as the city sleeps.
He knows
the small apartment of the
mother on Fifth Street,
how the brick crumbles
like her marriage did,
and how the stains on the walls cannot be covered.
He knows where her children go to school,
because she feels better
when he drives them.

She does not want to leave them alone to walk these streets
that are alive when the city sleeps.
He knows the man on the corner,
a silent journalist
and a professional watcher,
whose hands are stained with the ink
of other people's stories,
and the tears of other victims' families.
He knows the little girl
on the back road
in the small white house,
and that her favorite toy is a small stuffed mouse
that she left out in the rain
and still carries to the playground.
He knows the darkened streets,
he knows the people and their houses.
His route is etched into his skin
with the wrinkles on his hands
and printed in his mind
among his thoughts.
But tonight, the taxi driver
will meet someone new,
a puzzle to put together,
a story to learn.
He stops on the side of the road and waits
for the stranger to appear.
The night is open ahead of him,
filling the street like black fog

dotted with streetlights.
When the stranger appears,
they too are a shadow,
and fall into the backseat
without a word.
The taxi driver watches
the mystery in his backseat
and wordlessly starts the engine,
watching the headlights
cut through the dark.
The bar at the end of the road
with the sheets over the windows and
the broken door
is where the stranger came from.
The taxi driver knows
the building is so full of shadows
that sometimes the people within it become
shadows too.
A place like that can leave someone searching
for something that will never be found.
A place like that can be full of enough smoke
to chip and crack skin
like the worn yellow paint of his car.
The taxi driver's eyes wander
to the ghost in the backseat
with the unseeing eyes
and the twisted skin.
The taxi driver knows the city.

He knows that too many back roads

can lead a person to the dark

and can turn them into

a mystery.

He knows that smiles can be

stolen by the streets

that are alive when the city sleeps.

# winter song

The bricks were painted in a glaze of ice
and dotted with foggy reflections of streetlights,
warm sparks against the darkness
and the only light
to compete against the moon.
The stores were dark and empty
closed off against the cold
with tiny lights laced through the windows
to add a ghost of the holidays
to each dim corner of the block.
The night was gentle
but the air was harsh
and cut through our jackets to pinch our skin.
Our footsteps on the stone sidewalk
were the only sounds to break the silence of
the winter night.
Until you broke it too,
with one hand across the
strings of a guitar.

The cold was sharp enough to
steal the warmth from words
but you were not wearing gloves,
you were playing music.
We passed you
as you sat on the abandoned steps
in a corner in the dark,
filling the silence with your voice
and words that I didn't stay
long enough to understand.
Maybe it was too cold for you to be heard
because you were alone
but the moon was watching
and the streetlights glowed
and your lonely notes were sweet enough
to pause the creeping frost.
It was the night before Christmas Eve
and golden lights sparkled across the abandoned streets.
It had been a year of shadows,
but you brought a light,
and we didn't stop
to thank you.
We passed you again
and I know you saw us
but you didn't look up
and neither did we.
When we came to the corner again
it was silent

and your voice had been stolen
from the air
and the place where you had been sitting
was an empty shadow.
I do not know where you went;
maybe your hands were numb,
or the wind was drowning out your words
and you wanted to be warm.
Or maybe you thought
that the beauty you created
in the darkness and the cold
of that street corner
was never noticed
and we never told you
that it was.

# doors

The air is a spirit without mercy.
It can tear through clothing
and burn into skin,
and brand bodies with ice.
When it is cold enough,
the air can steal smiles from faces,
and hope from within.
The air can pull the last fluttering breath from lips.
The air can slice through a heart.
Not many people know the cold like she does.
She watches
as each month is stripped from the year,
uncovering a core
that is harsh and unforgiving.
The first snowflake to drift from the sky
and touch the sidewalk
is a joy
to the people walking home.
A smiling child with rosy skin and chocolate hair

laughs and opens his mouth
to catch a tiny frozen crystal on his tongue.
It seems the world has stopped to admire the beauty,
but as the snow lands on her skin
she notices the sting.
Winter settles over the city
as the days darken and fade to gray.
The chilled wind bites at our skin
through thick coats and mittens as we climb into cars,
and cuts through her tattered blanket.
For us,
the winter is a memory of fields frosted in snow
and happy pink-cheeked children
pulling sleds through a forest.
For her,
the winter is a memory of long nights and helpless shivers,
a memory of darkness and fingers blistered from cold.
She searches for shelter through the abandoned streets
as we close our doors against the howling wind
that sounds just like a monster.
She gathers her blanket around her
on the cold wooden bench as we sip hot drinks
and lean into the warmth of our bedsheets.
We rush home from our offices,
we stumble home from schools,
and we close our doors
against the burning cold air.
Yet in the subway,

on the sidewalks,

and in the stores,

people watch her without noticing

she has no door to close.

# the graffiti artist

She has filled the neighborhood with color,
color that can catch somebody by the eyes
and refuse to let go,
color that can overwhelm and embrace a body,
color that can feel
and touch
and leap,
color that can speak.
The figures she has painted on the walls
are still and silent against the brick
but in her thoughts they are loud,
in her thoughts they clamor for space in her mind
and battle to be freed through her colors.
Their enraptured eyes
and delicate bodies watch from the brick
as the girl's emerald hair hugs her neck
and her eyes focus through tortoiseshell glasses.
I know her as the graffiti artist,
the vibrant girl,

who was lonely until she befriended color.
Watching her arms glide across the walls
is a special kind of enchantment.
If you run a hand along the brick
you can feel the tears she left there.
If you watch the paintings move
you can see the family she longs for.
The woman painted blue in the corner is her mother,
always looking to the sky,
always reaching beyond the daughter before her,
always ready to fade.
When the old man in the yellow house
walks past the woman in blue,
he sees his sister
who gave him the ocean and retreated to the sky.
The goddess painted on the building across the street
is the girl who held the heart of the artist,
the girl who cried with her when she was lost.
The goddess is the artist's favorite
and she glows on the days when the artist
can barely summon a smile.
The graffiti artist lays her life across the buildings,
she gives us color
and makes us stop on the sidewalks as we walk to work
to wonder about the stories
buried beneath the paint.

# letters from the back of my mind (ii.)

# the art of being half asleep in an oversaturated room

I could rest my hand on the walls but I wouldn't be able
to feel. The light is overexposed and takes away my senses,
replacing them with an intangible hum of white noise.
My vision is marred with ghosts that hide behind the
closet doors of my mentality
and hover on the edge of consciousness.
It is always difficult to find the door
to this monotone room that is so uncomfortably bright.
My eyes are full, my hands
are empty, my heart
is blank, and I do not think of you.
If I listen, I can hear the pleading of my thoughts
to forget your face,
a dim apparition floating among the blankness
that seems to stretch for

eternity.
My eyelids fall and rise against the force of a thousand
empty hallways
as my questions lapse into static
and my fingers freeze
as if they're still tangled
in your hair.

# glass

I cannot look at the one who made you hate your skin
because if I did my eyes would pour with molten tears
and scald my porcelain face until it throbs
so I keep my eyes on the ribbons in my hands.
We have brought them to tie over your wounds.
You cannot hold your body,
so we will hold it for you as your limbs drift through the air
and you reach out for the purity of the clouds
as they paint you in a haze of dreams
and you cry oceans of silk
and you try to shatter your body of glass
with your murderous fists,
and we hold you as your thoughts pour from every crack,
and we tie the ribbons around your fingers,
as you whisper your wordless words,
as you twist in your body of glass.
You cannot feel your palms
as you lift them above your head,
as you inspect every crease and every foreign outline

and your transparent skin glints under the fading sun
and our ribbons cannot hold your broken glass.
You reach for the mirror in the sky
but we fight to cover your marble eyes
because the mirror will crush
your body of glass.

# december rain

remaining silent
among a chorus of sounds
is a lonely thing.
it is strange that one can be
lonely
in a room full of people
who caress your cheeks with their
smiles
and stroke your hair with their praise
and their questions of how you have been,
the question they continue to ask
and that you
continue to ponder.
remaining still
at an emptying amusement park
is a hollow thing.
it is nostalgia
as the lights announce their bold
flickering

solitary existence
to the blackness of the sky
while a song you heard once
drifts like an afterthought
from a speaker somewhere
to rest
lyricless
behind your heart and
to the left.
remaining wordless
in a dream
is a haunting thing
especially when it is
set at your old
elementary school
in hallways you do not recognize
but linger in your memory,
clinging to the walls of your mind
until you cry and stain the classroom floors,
a picture of what used to be.
keeping your eyes open
while only the city is awake,
remaining cold
while the earth warms,
sadness
is an odd thing–
the ghost of
December rain.

# you I see

Looking at you
wraps my wondering eyes in a coffin
as I am thrown like a child's forgotten toy across
the universe,
and the stars fall from the sky like fluorescent rain,
and the air that smells like the night
dances into my throat to stop my breath,
and I reach for the galaxy in your skin.
I want to find every planet and remember.
Looking at you
drags the oxygen from my lungs until I am nothing
as I am pulled like a strangled fish
into the bottom of the earth,
as the sun shudders in the sky and fights against the moon,
and the trees that once seemed gentle
creep towards me to push me farther from the clouds.
I reach for the stories in your eyes.
I want to find every word and remember.
Looking at you

hurts.

So why do I do it again?

# a note about tears

That stain bleeding across the ceiling could be a flower
or a face
I can't tell so I blink twice and the image blurs
and it's a face
she has full lips and a narrow neck and her mouth is open
she's crying and I hope she doesn't taste those tears
as I have because it's a strange thing
and tears don't belong on the tongue
I stare up at this woman on the ceiling among
tiles of an uncomfortable yellowed ivory
and decide to stand,
leaving her alone in the second stall
of a high school girl's restroom.
I do hope she keeps those tears
out of her mouth because that
makes them real.
I think
everyone should find a movie that makes them cry and
a person who doesn't.

# a picture of the playground at dusk

We wish for nightfall's numb grip in our chests
as the chain of the swing is cool beneath our fingertips,
leaving shallow imprints on our skin
and etching a picture on the back of our minds
of the playground at dusk.
It is a picture of you beside me
with no thoughts to break the silence.
It is a picture of the past,
beautifully stagnant in its glass frame.
Our hours pass under the weight of the present
as we become ghosts in our living rooms.
We let our minds wander enough to traverse the universe,
and we let them return with nothing.
Our thoughts catch us in a chokehold
that tightens with each scratch of a pencil,
each tap on a glaring screen,
each moment of empty existence.

Words of death become as light as a catchphrase on our lips,
as typical as a greeting.
We do not know what it feels like to stop being a person
so we never take them seriously.
In the back of our minds is our youth,
a flower we planted long ago
and forgot to water.
If we return to the swingset
I wonder if we will long to grasp the darkening sky
and twist the moonlight between our fingertips.
I wonder if we will laugh until our lungs ache
and our words fade.
I wonder if the air will drift through us
until we can feel autumn in our skin.
I wonder if our questions about the world will be as eternal
as our questions about ourselves.
I wonder if after all those years
we will still be breathing.
I wonder if we will still be living.
I wonder if we will still be young.

# a letter to the green princess

The hero in the books always wins the greatest prizes
and I once thought I was
I pulled her from the ground
and I promise I helped her grow
I did everything that I never ever could
I laced her hair in roses and traced art into her skin,
I told her beautiful stories and I kissed her garden eyes
until they closed
I held her when someone knocked the world
onto its side
and everything spilled and fell,
and the perfect things shattered.
But when I tore my heart out for her
when I trembled in her arms
I lost the greatest prizes
and I lost her pretty hands,
I fell and she would never catch me

and all my muted colors
but I am just a shell
and I am not the hero
and did I give her those bruises in her heart?
I thought I loved
I thought my eyes could tell her
I thought my thoughts told her so
I thought the sky that I gave her was enough
but do not love like that
because I am not the hero
and I am buried where she once stood.

# memories are not trustworthy things

I cannot find you.
I walk through the chambers of my mind,
each doorway a fleeting apparition,
and I run my torn fingers over the unfamiliar gashes
in the marble railing along
the stairs.
I know the stone is etched with your silhouette,
but I cannot find the words you wrote to me.
I cannot find the message scrawled across the staircase.
I do not walk anymore,
now I run,
frantically searching the empty streets
of my thoughts
as they wind into a twisted dreamland,
and my cries are never-ending,
as the road before me stretches into eternity,
and I do not know how to escape.

I am running

until the curve of your shoulder mars the blurry skyline.

I know you were a pretty thing,

but I cannot remember.

I cannot find you,

and I do not think I ever will.

# white birds

She does not hear the crack of the wood
as she watches the ceiling writhe above her.
She does not feel the burn of air down her throat,
in and out of her lungs that ache with dust,
as the walls tremble and collapse,
as the floor shakes and quivers like a wounded creature,
as her eyes close against the clouds in her mind,
as they threaten to wrap a string around her neck and pull
tight.
The shadows are here, reminders that walk
through the room to touch her face.
The shadows are here to breathe the past into her ears,
to numb her with every word.
As the room caves in to hug her body, she does not feel.
She only hears the muted chorus of her thoughts,
a melody dripping with regret.
Her mind flits between images as the plaster cracks
and falls like snow to the floor,
and she does not have a phone to call,

she does not have a hand to hold.
Her skin is broken
and her heart is tired
from hearing the comfort laced in lies,
her face is still among the broken house,
and only her thoughts are alive.
The bedsheets are heavy below her,
caked in the fallen paint.
The mirror is shattered and she would rip it apart
if it stood.
She sees them swarming ahead of her,
the white birds flitting across her vision,
the memories screaming in her eyes.
She does not hear the house crumbling
as the white birds shake in the air,
as the white birds come down to sing sweet songs
and rip her skin,
as the white birds call to her and she cannot stay still,
as the white birds tear into her heart
to rest where her mind cannot find them.

# I remember you

It lurks behind every wall
and in every corner of the house.
I cannot tell if it is a person, or if it is only a nameless force
pulling me back to the past.
It arrived with the cool wind of autumn,
and it follows me as I walk from room to room.
It speaks to me,
telling me I am ashamed of it,
telling me I am ignoring it.
It tells me to pick up the phone,
and when I do not,
it leaves.
It leaves,
only to return again the next day,
lurking
and begging
and hurting.
I convince myself that I do not know who the figure is,
even though I know the pain

and I know the words.
Whenever I try to look it in the face,
I see that year.
I had been young,
and I had been trapped.
I want the figure to leave,
but pain drips off of it like water,
leaving a trail that I step into.
The figure follows me,
crying lies all over the floor,
flooding the house with a broken venom that fills my lungs
and makes me stay.
I want to run away from this figure
that has found its way back from the past
and crawled into my house
to haunt the walls.
I sit down at the table to write
and feel the touch of its cold hands
when I don't ask for it.
I scream and tell it to go away
because I will never be silent again.
I scream as it tells me it is sorry,
and that it is hurting,
and that I am helping.
It leaves through the back door
and I am alone for the afternoon hours.
I know it is in other houses,
haunting other walls

and embracing other people in a sad longing.
It tells me I am the only one,
but I am one house among many,
one face among others,
the same helpless skin as five more.
I do not want it back,
but the figure knocks on my door
and cries a puddle of venom again
before I can send it away forever.

# letter to the girl that I (don't) know best

It's been a while since we've talked.
Yesterday I caught you sitting with crossed legs
on the living room floor
playing that song we used to like
on repeat, twelve times,
waiting to drown yourself in the unforgiving waters of
nostalgia and a painting of youth.
I caught you curling your hair with a rose-colored blade,
your pupils etched with words you have never once said.
I know your eyes are greener when you cry.
I know you don't like the
definable but unknowingly are always searching
for descriptions and answers.
Tell me, why did you bury your thoughts in her name
while waiting for her
to love you? Sometimes I wonder
why you never give up, my unrelenting

friend, my enigmatic
persona that I thought I knew.
I wonder why you fell in love with
her for her face and her laugh
and him for his eyes and his questions
and why you now avoid thinking about them both.
I wonder why you worry so much about wasting the
present but you can't get your mind out of the
future and your heart out of the past.
Could you tell me why you've always believed in ghosts?
It must be strange to ponder the existence
of things you can't see
but I guess that's how it works
with things like love and pain.
I know half of you is nearly asleep against the
stars in a red velvet dress, whispering words to a song you
played the day before, with a flower tucked behind your ear,
a book open in your palm and a poem
in your chest.
I know the other half of you is running
through the city holding someone's hand, yelling about
the music you can hear in the distance
and the way the streetlights
make the sky darker and the world larger.
You've always followed Time and begged her for more, or
for less, depending on the day.
Time intervenes and carries change
like a weapon on her back. If it is a Saturday,

you run to meet her.
If it is a Tuesday, you hide in the hallway
where all of your memories
hang in picture frames.
I guess that's how it works with you, a double-edged sword.
You always know what to write and not what to say.
You always know how to help and not how to ask for it.
You cradle emotion
to your chest like a gift, drawing it from people's
mouths and then accepting it, carrying it with you and
caring for it until it matures and can carry itself.
Emotion should be held in the sweetest of chambers,
but your own is made of iron and steel
and filled with water, ever-changing.
You love stories and never find the time to read them.
You crave the city but never talk to its people.
I'm starting to think
that among all of the questions that you ask
you will never answer all of mine
so for now I will watch you frozen
in the mirror.

# inescapable thoughts from the middle of the night

I.
I do not know what love is
and I do not think you do either.
We can wrap gentle words around it
until it is tied tightly to be examined,
until it thrashes violently
against the bindings of description,
against the chains of tangibility.
We can tangle our fingers in the pain
and return alone and stained red,
announcing that we know what love is,
but we do not.
I do not know if love
is the way she looks at her,
or the way their hands are woven together,

or an amber lock of hair on a picnic blanket,
or a letter filled with stories
that nobody else would understand.
I do not know if love is the sob
that will course through her body
and scream in her veins
the day that her lover reaches into someone else's eyes
and comes back with a flower etched into her skin
and a longing to disappear.
Or maybe there will be no sobs
and no longing to disappear.
Maybe those two girls will be careful
with each other's hearts
and will stay together like the couple next door.
The couple next door
yells late into the night,
kicking furniture,
clawing at doors until they slam
in each other's faces,
and until silence settles when the sun rises,
when she goes to work
and he sleeps
and loses the time.


II.
I do not know what heartbreak is,
and I know you say that you do
but you don't,

because you claim your heart has been shattered
and is made of glass
when it still beats inside of you
and I could touch the proof
with a finger to your throat
and the rhythmic whisper of your pulse against my skin.
Yet you say that it is broken
and you want someone to collect the shards,
but I do not understand
because a heart cannot form shards.
You said that somebody reached into your chest
and tore your heart apart
and left you with this broken glass,
but I do not believe you.
I do not believe you
because the heart is buried in your skin
and the ribcage holds your heart
right there with your lungs
so they cannot be stolen.
Or maybe I do believe you
because love can snake through the ribcage
and drain the heart
and puncture the lungs
until you will always ache.

III.
I do not know if love is beautiful.
You told me once that it is

but I can see what it has done to you.
If I ignore the bruises that love left in your eyes,
then maybe love is a heavenly thing.
Maybe love is etched into the lines of your mother's smile
or in the infinite arms of the trees
forever grasping for sunlight
or in the murmur of the water
cascading like jewels across
unforgiving rock.
If I ignore the ghosts that it left
to whimper in your picture frames
and wail in your hallways,
maybe love is a pretty thing.
Maybe love is the way the sky caresses the windows at dusk
or maybe it is a song to dance to
barefoot in the living room
until it pulses through the floor
and wraps your mind in a symphony of delicate thoughts
that pull tears from your eyes.
Maybe love is the way she
always kisses her envelopes before she seals them.


IV.
I do not know what it means to love
a person's face
or the way a person talks
or the way they fold their hands
or the way they smile when they listen to you.

You said you used to know how it feels
to look at someone with love
and I believe you.
I do not know if love is
the way someone's laughter can make you wonder if
they could paint a galaxy on the ceiling with their voice.
I do not know if love is
looking at someone and remembering
the things you thought you would forget,
looking at someone and wondering if their eyes
have always reflected a canvas of untouchable color,
or if maybe you just never noticed it before.
I do not know if love is
losing breath when you see someone
because you will never grow tired of their face.
I do not know if love is
knowing someone
whose smile is
the way the wind tangles your hair
when you lean out of the car window at night
and wish you could touch
the city lights.

V.
I still do not know what love is,
but I know that I love you.

# unknown address

Memories are the ghosts of thought.
Memories will kiss the corners of your mind,
but disappear when you reach out
to tug them closer.
Memories are faded pictures.
Memories will appear in broken fragments,
some of them so vivid
you could dip your fingers in the color.
Others so far away,
you can only feel their footprints.
Memories are thieves when they vanish
and take the past with them.
I have forgotten her,
but never how the droplets of sunlight
used to cling to her eyelashes,
or the way she could crochet
a blanket out of words to fall asleep in,
or the way her laughter was more quiet
than the moonlight,

or the way her eyes were two fragments of the sky.
I have forgotten her,
almost,
but memory leaves me letters on the stairs.

# conversation between someone who believes in fate and someone who believes in fact

I can tell that
your breath tastes like nostalgia when you look at me.
My lungs hurt because they are so full of you
and your existential words screaming of a lost cause.

> No, my breath tastes like the soda
> you bought last night, because you gave some
> to me and it refused to leave my tongue.
> I've never been inside your lungs,
> and my words have never been anywhere
> except for your ears.

You're lying.

When the night falls like a wish
across the dollhouse suburbs
you cry because you miss the way I drew poems
from your lips
like sparkling water infused with roses.
You miss the way you used to search for
memories so much that you forgot to
create them.

I don't miss you.
I hate the way you speak like that.
I want to rip the fancy words from your mouth.
The only thing you drew from my lips
was a wish to leave.
Will you let me sleep without hearing your voice?

'Will you let me sleep without hearing
your voice?'
My voice always fit in your hands better
than my fingers did,
no wonder you can't forget it.

That's not what I meant.

You always try to take back what you say.
The moment the words leave your mouth
you swallow them again.

I've always wanted you to speak
without regretting so much.

        I've always wanted you to speak without thinking so
        much.

Did you leave me because my eyes reflected yourself,
but showed you laminated in shame?
You didn't forget me when you left me,
I can tell by the hesitation of your breath
and how it pauses before it leaves your lips.

        I left you because you made me tired.
        My breath doesn't hesitate, I have a head cold.

Do you remember when I spent the entirety
of a silver November morning
wrapping you a gift using twenty dollar wrapping paper
laced in glitter
from the store down the street?

        No.

Do you remember?

        Yes.

Do you remember how I cried when you
didn't accept it?

> Yes. And I cried when I got home.

You did what?

> I do miss you sometimes.

# untitled

If you untangled my thoughts from my body,
would I float?
Would my questions become your oxygen,
invisible echoes of what I once was,
life that you drink from the air to feed your own?
Would I be the wind that clings to the trees
until they surrender their leaves?
Would I be the captivating whisper of the moonlight
along the pavement
as the sky closes its eyes?
Would I be the lyrics you have forgotten,
hiding on the edges of your consciousness?
The door to the closet in my mind will not close,
it is overflowing with wonders that only you
would understand.
I know that you could unravel me with your eyes.
But if you stripped me to nothing and took away my skin,
what would I be?

# seeing ghosts (iii.)

# strange stories from 1992

Ms. Johnson was the woman who lived
down the street from us.
I remember that delicate town without a name,
as blank as a primrose.
She would move in when winter pulled her in through the
back door
and locked it behind her.
Ms. Johnson gave the little girls bows for their hair,
she tied them tightly
and arranged the curls
until the neighborhood was full of dolls.
That was what she called them as they begged
for hot chocolate.
Ms. Johnson did not worry
when they spilled it on their dresses,
she did not worry as the stain sprawled
across their chests like

a bleeding chocolate flower,
Ms. Johnson always had a spare dress
and a way to remove the stain.
I visited her one gray Saturday in January
and as the monotone light clung to my cheeks I
climbed her front steps.
She opened the door without a knock and smiled,
her voice a pleasant trill that shaped my name
as if she had said it many times before.
I didn't ask for something sweet
because momma didn't let me taste sweet
because she thought it hurt my teeth.
Ms. Johnson placed a sour candy on my tongue
and asked me if I was going to church tomorrow
because that would reassure momma and make her
less worried when I left the house at dusk in search of
nothing in particular.
I told Ms. Johnson that sour candy was my favorite
and I loved the way the sour
dissolves into sweetness over time
but leaves your tongue
hurting until you can taste
nothing else.
I told her that I used to sneak it into school
under my sleeves
and offer it to my newest friends
back when momma gave me sour candy
before father told her it was bad for my health.

Ms. Johnson got very serious then
and her ballet voice descended into a whisper
as she told me that father wasn't home
as she told me that father wasn't ever coming home again
as she told me that I could sing in the house now,
as she told me that I wouldn't understand but that
momma would be grateful,
so grateful that I wouldn't have to hear her nighttime tears
tracing landscapes into the walls.
Ms. Johnson told me that I am a beautiful doll
with pretty brown curls,
and I do not need to worry anymore.
I can have as much candy as I want.
I took a handful of sour candy,
as tart as a forgotten dream.
I walked out onto the porch to see five other doll girls
waiting
to visit Ms. Johnson for
hot chocolate and a smile.
I crossed the street and opened our front door
allowing the January gray to follow me in
allowing it to see the house for the first time
allowing it to seep into the empty space
allowing it to embrace me
because father wasn't home
and neither was I.

# stay away from the night garden

My flower is crying among the grass
My flower is screaming for my hands
My flower is dying
as the unknown thing creeps through the garden.

The unknown thing has a twisted body and a broken back
The unknown thing looks at me
and smiles.

My flower is burning under the red sky
My flower is flailing in the dirt
I would reach out to touch its crumbling skin
but the twisted thing hangs in the air before my flower
watching me and smiling.

My flower has pulled her roots from the ground,
they once accepted water and now it seeps out

leaving her arms fragile as they reach for me.
I cannot look at my flower.
I cannot look at the unknown thing.

My flower's eyes are fluttering like flies without wings
My flower's petals are weak.
I fall into the garden
and the unknown thing smiles.

My flower is dying
My flower is dying
My flower is dead.

# pretty girl,
# haunting me

You want to play make believe
and you want me to be the one with silk for eyes
so you can be the one with copper petals for hair
and you can sing songs about love and blood
and all of the red things
into my ears
until they haunt me past the darkness
when I sleep in the cold place.
And when your hair glows like you want it to
we can play house
and you can be the sister
and I can feed you mysteries on a plate of curiosity until
you will stop asking me questions
about why my eyes are made of silk
and why the silk is stained.
So you want to play hide and seek
and when I turn my back

I can feel the gentle bite of your gaze

until it chases me into the room in the back

when the teeth sink deeper

and I kneel beneath the bed to cover myself

with the floorboards

until you cannot see me

or my silk eyes

so you will have to hate me instead.

# weeds in the soil

It is cold and fine and falls from her hands
like water that leaves a stain.
She could bury her fingers in it until she
is under the ground too,
swallowed from the universe
and plunged into the depths of all that is unreal,
left to swim among the darkness, left to be still
among the breathing and fluid
among the dead,
out of breath when her only one lies below her.
She piles it into her hands, digging
until she can reach an answer that will never appear,
pulling at the questions like weeds in the dirt.
She can feel him moving, she can feel him breathing
and she can feel his heart
even though he is still in the soil and she will be too.
It is filling her lungs
and she welcomes the blankness of her mind,
the feeling in her fingertips

of dull pain and sharp memory,
the soil building up around her like a wall,
a fortress that she cannot break down
but she will, and she feels her face
as she falls into the ground,
because she is not beautiful anymore
and she wants to feel what he felt when he fell,
so she will take the step and bury herself
in the soil that breathes
until she cannot.

# murderous sky

The air hangs limp over the streets,
bleeding the cries of decaying dreams onto the windows
as the sky shrieks with a distant song.
The infection is planted in the root of every tree
and snakes through the town until each door is locked.
To take a step into the street
where the people are silent and the sky screams
is enough to twist a heartbeat until it races
or pale a face until it is paper.
The headlines and the aching words
are whispered through the cracks in the walls
and slide through the storm drains
to reverberate
under the shoes of those who dare to face the sky.
The memories of the lost
wind around every home
and knit the town into a blanket of sorrow,
sewing each trembling lip into stillness
and crocheting each teardrop

into the fabric of the deafening sky.
The games are hushed and the toys are broken
as the silence suffocates the children
who fall asleep taken captive by nightmares
of the ghosts who haunt the streets
with the metal eyes and foreign mouths,
but these ghosts
do not vanish with the daylight.
The woman in the upstairs window
of house twenty-eight
rests a hand on the glass
and imagines it in pieces.
She looks to the sky
and imagines it collapsing
to conceal the agony
and the muted colors
and the silent words
and the tense bodies
and the unblinking eyes
so she pulls her curtains closed
as the country cries.

# mary jean

She'll tie a ribbon around my wrist and pull it tight
until my blood thrums decisively
and threatens to break my skin,
until it threatens to form the river
that she promised we would visit
when I was old enough to walk down the street on my own
at night
and when she was old enough
to escape my mind.
She'll tie a ribbon around my waist and braid it
gently,
so that I will not notice it if I am still.
She'll whisper stories in my ears and laugh like peace,
as if she is the flower and I am the light.
She only visits me when I dream,
but if she begs enough
I will see her face in the reflection of the water
right there
staring back at me with the moon.

She'll tie a ribbon around my palm and
paint my fingernails red,
and warn me about the wide eyes at night,
the ones that have followed me home from the candy store
where the owner gives me a lollipop
just to see me smile.
She'll warn me about the wide eyes
that are painted in the window.
She'll tie a ribbon around my ankle and kiss my cheek
until my view of her is melted in a kaleidoscope
of nightmares,
and my thoughts are in agony,
and I threaten to wake up.
She'll tie a ribbon around my neck and wrap it twice
until my breath is a flailing and hopeless creature
that scrambles from my throat like a ghost.
She'll smile at my burning skin
and my frantic heart,
and she'll watch me fight to catch the hope
dangling from her fingertips,
clutched between thumb and forefinger,
the pretty pink thing
that is laced with silken tears.
She'll drag the hope away
and I will remind her who I am.
I will tell her that I am a girl with a story to write,
and someone once told me that my smile was
fit for illustration.

I will tell her that I am a girl with a life of my own,
and she'll freeze the words on my lips
and drag a clawed fist through my hair
and whisper
*"darling,*

*you are me."*

# optophobia

She climbs into the depths of her mind,
hiding in the lucid layers of silk darkness,
crouching in the shadows.
She pulls the curtains against her,
letting them tangle around her neck.
She swallows the visions of all she has seen
and the blurry images scald her throat.
The prying chorus of voices crawls across her skin,
the neighbors whispering stories,
so she finds the crack of the window in the wall
and drags it down onto the hazy voices underneath,
leaving them to beg for air
as they suffocate.
Her invisible fingers splayed wide
are creatures
as they find her faded face
and her eyes that will never open.
She can hear her veins as they wander through her skin,
she can hear her thoughts as they scream in their cages,

she can hear what she once saw.
The vicious laughter of life tears across her ears
as she stares into the darkness with her
eyes that will never open.
The dark things are her favorites,
the velvet hearts and the soft breath.
They join her in her hiding place
to keep the sight away
as it slithers down the street, holding hands with light,
and carrying a bouquet of yellow flowers.
She thought she buried those lovely yellow blossoms
in the earth that night
with her eyes.
Her eyes have been taken by her own gentle fingers
and the visions only haunt her in her dreams,
when she dreams
that she can breathe,
and when she dreams
that she is alive.

# eisoptrophobia

I can see my face in the glass,
torn skin with foreign eyes,
as my cheeks peel away from my veins,
and my heart scrambles from my chest.
I can see my face but it is not mine.
I can see the mirage in my dreams,
every wall is a specter as they descend upon my skin,
and the ceiling cascades down in silver droplets
like water,
sliding into my eyes until I cannot see the girl in the glass.
I drown as the walls and their agonized faces
press into my own and breathe my only breath.
I can see her as she stands in the corner of the hallway,
I can see the distorted children dancing behind me,
I can see the air flailing as it is pulled into my lungs,
I can see the paint melting from the walls.
I can see the glass at the end of the hallway
smiling at me.

# somniphobia

She knows
that if you open your mouth under the surface of reality
you will never be heard
and your soundless scream will echo in your ears
until you can only hear the static whispers
and lethal fragments of words
as they sweetly sing you to sleep.
She knows
that the unknown darkness of the mind is strangely familiar
as the shadow fingers fold against the door
and watch you from the closet
and all of the flowers in the garden long to hear your heart
as their silhouettes drag across the walls.
She knows
that the cloaked one will sing you to sleep
even if you leave the light on,
and you will see the twisted lucid pictures in your mind
when your eyelids stop fighting against the insistent fingers
and your lungs will fill with the dark ocean

and you will not remember how to move your arms.

She knows

that if you stay with the cloaked one

for too long

you will never wake up.

# people watching (iv.)

# emaline

She has beads on her shoelaces,
one of every color,
and scribbles in the margins of her notebook paper.
She has full waves of orange hair,
and twists the strands around her fingers
when somebody looks at her,
or talks to her,
or asks her if she is listening,
because she never is.
She has a world in her mind,
and her dreams live in the glass fortress
of make-believe.
She has thoughts that whisper stories
into her ears,
as she paints them onto a canvas.
She has a world in her mind
where her father never lost himself in a bottle
and the floorboards never shook
and the walls never reverberated

her mother's fearless words
that cut through
Daddy's false facade.
She has a world in her mind
where her parents, together
will touch her hair and tell her
"Emaline,
we are going
home"
and she won't have to guess
which one.

# rosalyn

I listen to the crescendo of your voice as it pulls me
through the crowded streets.
Your words intertwine with the air,
unfolding a story so intricate
that it trails behind you like green tulle,
vibrant against the fading light.
A man passes us, and you inform me
that his monotone blazer
means he works in an office
and plays with numbers for fun,
and that his wife has never seen him laugh.
If he did laugh, it would sound as raw and unfamiliar
as the voice of a stranger.
I nod, because you are the type of person
to paint pictures out of letters
and color coordinate your pens,
and fill your drink with sugar
until you forget how bitter tastes.
I am the type of person who knows

that even when we spend our lives
chasing an improbable future
and even when we achieve it,
we all look the same to the universe.
I glance at your full eyes, lined in purple, as you
twirl a strand of hair around your thumb.
I want to hear all of your observations,
as your fingers trace the outline of the clouds
against the setting sun that peers at us through skyscrapers.
I notice that you added pins to your backpack,
a moon, a rose, and a rainbow.
I would like to tell you how much I love the details of you.
I stop on the sidewalk with my eyes squinted to the skyline,
because I have forgotten the day I met you.
Maybe I never remembered it anyway,
because time has buried it in my mind,
but today the blankness feels different
among the chaos in the air and the vividness of you.
You tilt your head at my silence and tug my hand,
asking strawberry-flavored questions
that you tuck behind my ear
with my hair.
I do not answer them,
but I know that if I did, you would make up a story
about the day I met you, making it as dramatic as possible
until I laugh.
Sometimes I wonder how I look to you.
When I ask, you tell me that I look like

the sky before a storm,
or the music your favorite record plays,
or streetlights after midnight.
I nod along with you,
wondering if I will ever see myself
as the person you describe.
I don't know where you find your stories,
but I want to write them down and read them
again and again
until I understand every word
like I'm a girl inside your head.

# sasha

He wears himself out on a banner,
bright and shimmering, made of golden thread.
When he hides from the cold
it is draped around his shoulders,
and he holds it above his head to meet the sky.
Everyone can see it, and some smile as they reach out
to ponder the color.
Although some of them do not, and some of them run.
Some of them laugh at the beautiful banner,
and some of them whisper things he will never hear.
But everyone can see Sasha's banner.
There are some who pull at the fabric
until the banner cries to him,
torn and aching at a lost shining thread.
Sasha will lay the banner on the grass,
carefully kneel beside it,
and mend the open wound.
His tears blend with the gold
and nobody will notice,

so Sasha holds his banner high again.

All of himself on the banner,

it catches the wind and he smiles.

His skin sprinkled in freckles is turned to the sun,

wherever he wanders, the banner follows.

People hold the edges, examining the scars

and admiring the glow.

The children downtown sing and smile for Sasha,

their tiny hands grabbing for the sparkling gold.

Their eyes will light with wonder,

and Sasha will stop to sit beside them.

They will ask about the banner,

and Sasha will give them each a thread.

They do not know how to weave it,

but he knows they will learn.

One day the sky will be full of beautiful banners.

# violette

Your fingers are splayed against the violet clouds of dusk
as the sky folds against your skin
and your laughter cascades across me.
I watch as the sounds of the quiet lives
and the forbidden stories
wind through your hair
and breathe their words into your luminous mind.
We are silent
until there is nothing but the promise
whispering.
So I turn to meet my eyes to yours
enigmatic
but I know them now
as the fluorescent stars toss and turn
like toy boats
in an ocean sky.

# sabine

I saw her
in the bookstore
where shadows cling to pages.
She was
silhouetted in wordless songs
and was leaning over to brush her finger across
the saddest story
in the aisle.
She carried an abstract longing as a veil
as she looked out of the window
and watched a film unravel against the glass,
when all I could see was the reflection
of her carmine lips
breathing delicate enrapturement onto
the blankness.
There was not one person there
who hadn't noticed her.
There was not one person there
who had ever seen

the sun and the moon
meet
to create a person,
with a fortress of air in her heart
and a deep red story of sorrow on her lips,
Sabine.

# elliot

The pavement tore his knee
and he caught the street with his palms,
his eyes filling with tears
and his mouth opening in a silent scream.
He was too young to know,
so he cried with his sister and he stared at his knee,
scared by the stark streak of blood against his skin.
Nobody widened their eyes at the teardrops on his cheeks,
tiny rivers hiding in his memory.
He stood and dried the rivers with a cloth,
because boys don't cry.
He grew until he could hear the voices.
When he presses his fingers to his ears,
the words crawl under his skin.
When his chest aches from the weight,
and his eyelids shake and his fists clench,
he lifts his face to the sky
and hopes that the gray torrents of rain
will conceal the broken rivers on his cheeks

because boys don't cry.
He stands before his closet and pulls half of it to the ground,
tangling his hands with the clothing,
watching himself bury it
and throw his favorite things away,
clawing at the fabric as if he is someone else,
as if he doesn't know himself,
because they told him that if he wore it
he would never be a man.
And he listened,
and he hopes he can forget
the time he found his first job
and bought that shirt with the money.
He hopes he can forget that it was his favorite,
because boys don't cry.
He closes his bedroom door,
fingers shaking on the lock,
because the words say he is weak
and his heart cannot breathe,
because he doesn't see life as a fight
to be won with fists and swords and disrespect.
Beautiful Elliot with his fingers on the lock,
willing himself to be a statue of a boy,
strong and unmoving,
never breathing and never hurting.
Broken Elliot with his fingers on his mouth,
because he has to hide as his skin breaks and his heart pours
because nobody should see his weakness.

Elliot is silent as he throws himself against the wall,

as he tears the shining necklace from his throat

because he can never be strong if he looks like a woman.

Elliot is silent as his mind burns a hole in his skin,

because he could never tell them

the thoughts that cloud his head

because boys don't cry.

Please,

Elliot, with your guarded eyes,

with your broken rivers and your favorite shirt,

please do not shield your thoughts with the rain.

Do not lock yourself in your bedroom,

do not fear the words,

and let yourself show

because boys do cry.

# ivan

The velvet fur of a toy lion touches his fingertips
as he wraps his sheets around the purple paint
as he waits for the footsteps on the stairs
and counts off on his fingers all the things he said
and did not say,
and all the things he did,
and all the flaws she saw,
because any one of them
could be covered by a stroke of purple paint
or a crimson word of venom in his ear.
The map on his skin could lead a stranger on a road trip
to his past and his present,
even if not all the scars are visible.
He used to remember them all,
and the purple paint faded but the
pain never did.
He would crack a picture frame
he would spill her water on the stairs
and she would paint him in purple,

and it stung,

it stung,

it stings.

The little lion is strong in the dark

and Ivan sees himself

in another place where she is not waiting at home

in another place where he can run far

in another place where he can feel the mist of dusk

kiss his weary skin

in another place where he can heal.

He kisses the fur before she opens the door,

he presses his cheek to the mane,

and he tells himself he will ignore

the burning flower she could plant on his cheek

and the way his skin wishes it could revolt but can't,

so it lets the sharp things in.

He is almost as tall as her

but she has a ghost lifting her up to seep over him

with purple.

He is not a child anymore

he is not a little lion

but she is still the purple ghost.

He looks up to the ceiling

and watches the shadows dance without moving,

and looks down at the stuffed toy

questioning time

because when she bought him the lion

she was kind.

# luca

I had a strange dream last night
you were there and you had a new tattoo
on your finger but I didn't ask what it meant
I knew you had probably tattooed it yourself
the night before during one of your
creative episodes
I remember what you said
"the city is a canvas painted with people's faces"
or
"the universe is a coalescence of our collective
thought, dusted in stars made up by the words
we cannot say."
The last time you had a new tattoo
you told me that you couldn't
sleep because you were
watching the moon and Saturn write
each other love letters.
In this dream I couldn't feel your hand in mine
but I could hear you crying

I could hear you telling me
"five o'clock is the saddest hour of the day"
I would agree because that is the hour
when I always think of you
the artist
in the back of the room with your pen making line drawings
"the walls were
white and I
was gray and I couldn't
feel your hand
in mine."

# dear society, (v.)

# she

Words,
winding around her throat,
taking her breath and replacing it with quiet venom.
She cannot speak, she cannot scream,
she cannot change the way they look.
She cannot stop the words,
the way they used to strangle her,
the way they used to suffocate her
and make her burn.
The way she now walks through them without blinking.
They way they surround her, and the way she could
crush them until they have no sound left to make,
cut them until each letter screams in agony,
pull them apart until they crack and the greed
bleeds onto the sidewalk,
but they would never be gone.
Her life, years of buried pain that nobody
dares to acknowledge,
has been spent concealing what she cannot hide,

apologizing for herself and her skin that is
pale and smooth as the pink petals of a rose,
her hair that flows like the finest silk
and is less expensive.
They have told her to cover the body that gives her life,
and the skin she breathes in,
because skin is an invitation
and she is the reward.
They tell her she is responsible for the eyes that follow her,
creeping lower and consuming the body that isn't hers,
surrounding her in whispers that clench her teeth
and make her walk faster.
They measure her skirt with a ruler
and tell her that the fault is hers,
because less clothing means more of a distraction
and less of a human.
She paints herself in armor every day,
fighting a war that nobody seems to notice.
They give sympathetic frowns when they hear the stories
of hands and screams and darkness.
Yet they are silent on the sidewalk,
averting their eyes when the words begin.
They are afraid to speak of the truth that unfailingly
follows her.
She has been told to hide,
she has been told to run, she has been told to
obey, she has been told to quiet her voice, she has been
told she is weak, she has been told she is dramatic,

she has been told it could be worse.

She has been told she is a woman.

She is a woman who will never be silent again.

# forgotten planet

Words scrawled across the stones,
plastic floating in the breeze like flower petals,
tangling in the grass and piling in masses,
wrapping the earth in a coffin.
She breathes, and the plastic forms a mask,
suffocating, and hugging tight against the green.
The birds land and stumble among the debris,
watching another car arrive to add to the pile,
watching the earth take another cautious breath.
Thrown away without a second thought,
crushed without hesitation,
forgotten as if it is harmless,
left to rest on her surface,
left to wander among her air.
Among the pieces of nothing,
below the ripped tire and among the broken plastic,
a new pulse beats, of a different kind.
It breathes in the beauty of sky
as it stretches up through the dirt,

and it breathes in the poison of plastic.

A nodding yellow head among gray and black,

leans to the sun and takes a tired breath with the earth.

# shoelaces

The shoelaces used to be white,
they used to be new and they used to be clean.
The strings are stained with dirt,
they are now worn and frayed,
but they are just as strong,
she knows.

The shoelaces came with him.
They were held by the air in the doorway,
sliding into her house like tiny snakes,
harmless.

The boy with shoes without laces
used to be nice,
he used to be new and he used to be clean.
He used to whisper pretty things
and his silhouette looked like a promise
under the archway.

As the pretty things turn to poison
and the fingers turn to claws
and the ache turns to burn turns to agony,
and he plants the clouds in her mind,
as the shoelaces are stained with their
collective thoughts,
and the shoelaces are stained with her skin
as she thinks of his words,
as she thinks of his lovely eyes and his horrible face.


She shuts the door


He will creep under


She closes her windows


His breath slides through the cracks in the walls
like the tiny snakes hovering in the air
suspended
and waiting,


And she reaches for the tiny snakes,
and he pulls her down
and the shoelaces fall from the air
and twist around her neck
to stop the racing thoughts,
to leave a mark of dirt
and to take away the light.

# poison

The poison on her breath is flowing through her veins,
coiling in venomous ringlets in her blood.
It is spreading like a disease through her limbs,
suffocating her mind,
blurring her vision.
The poison is bitter in the bottle,
catching the light and glinting an amber smile.
The poison is numb on her tongue and thick on the rim,
warm in her skin and hot in her lungs,
drowning in her stomach and pulsing through her muscles.
Her body is limp and could drop from the poison,
her mind could wander away with her breath,
and her heart could never return.

# beautiful silver

The wide eyes see nothing,
the streetlights swarm
against the fluid darkness,
and bleed to paint the windshield in a glittering picture
of orange tears.
The weak hands hold nothing,
and the fingers shake and tremble with the lethal current
that runs through them,
filling the veins with something deadly and electric,
pulling crying droplets of water from the skin
that mix with the scent of
a heart worn and cracked.
The shadow street expands to the black horizon,
reaching up like a hand that will never be touched,
creeping higher to mix with the heavy clouds.
The air is thick with the breath of the night,
and the sky aches and shifts above the highway.
The other pair of eyes watches carefully,
accepting the aching sky as beautiful,

turning up the velvet melody on the radio.
Hair winds around her neck in perfect ringlets,
golden in the reflection of the lights,
drifting out the window and hovering along her shoulders.
The fine silver thread glistens around her neck,
draped like moonlight against her skin.
She thinks of the photo folded inside the locket,
she thinks of the smiles she will return to,
and she looks to the aching sky.
And the sky looks down, and the sky sighs.
The wide eyes do not see, the hands do not feel,
the heart beats but the breath never follows.
The wheel under the trembling fingers slips away.
The muscles tense and tangle under the skin,
running without motion.
The sky looks down, and the sky cries
As the necklace shines and the foot slams down,
As the muscles shake and the car flies,
As the mouth opens and the heart pauses,
As the pavement yells under the loud darkness,
As the people slow and time follows,
As the photo pales among the chain.
The sky looks down, and the sky screams
As the silver chain twists and the hair flies,
As the trembling hands slow,
As the metal is torn like paper,
As the steel is crushed like bones,
As the bones splinter like shattered wood.

And the sky looks down, and the sky dies,

As the darkness fills the air,

As it pushes through the streetlights,

As her hair is loose among the glass

As the fingers are still,

As the skin is open,

As the shattered heart creeps slowly,

As the cars are folded on the street,

And the beautiful silver chain remains
below them.

The tangled hair,

the still hands,

and the beautiful silver.

# the listening stream

Strands of delicate light hang across the leaves
like shifting decorations against green.
Below the canopy,
water murmurs and whispers against the rock,
creating a song that can only be heard in silence.
The surface glistens
and flows to merge with the thoughts of those who pass it,
luminescent under the breath of dusk,
speaking gentle words
that cannot be heard unless
one looks deeper
than every moment
before.

# *about the author*

*Photo Credit: Violette Smith*

Malia Robinson is a current high school student, poet, and violinist living in New England. When she isn't studying or frantically completing math problems, she spends her time daydreaming and contemplating unanswerable questions. In the 2021 Scholastic Art and Writing Awards, her poems "A Picture of the Playground at Dusk," "Pretty Girl, Haunting Me," "Shoelaces," "Weeds in the Soil," and "Winter Song" received Honorable Mention regional awards. Her poem "Emaline" received the Silver Key award.

Printed in the USA
CPSIA information can be obtained
at www.ICGtesting.com
LVHW012153170124
769269LV00041B/1924